This Book Belongs To:

- - - - - - - - - - - - - - - -

First Published in 2025 by Puddle Publishing
Text Copyright © H.G Puddle
Illustration Copyright © H.G Puddle

Email: hg.puddle@gmail.com

ISBN: 978-1-0686212-4-6

For L.D.S
Special thanks to Kate & Guy

Let me introduce you all to Bob –
A man who really loves his job.

For thirty years he's served the zoo
And done the best job he can do.

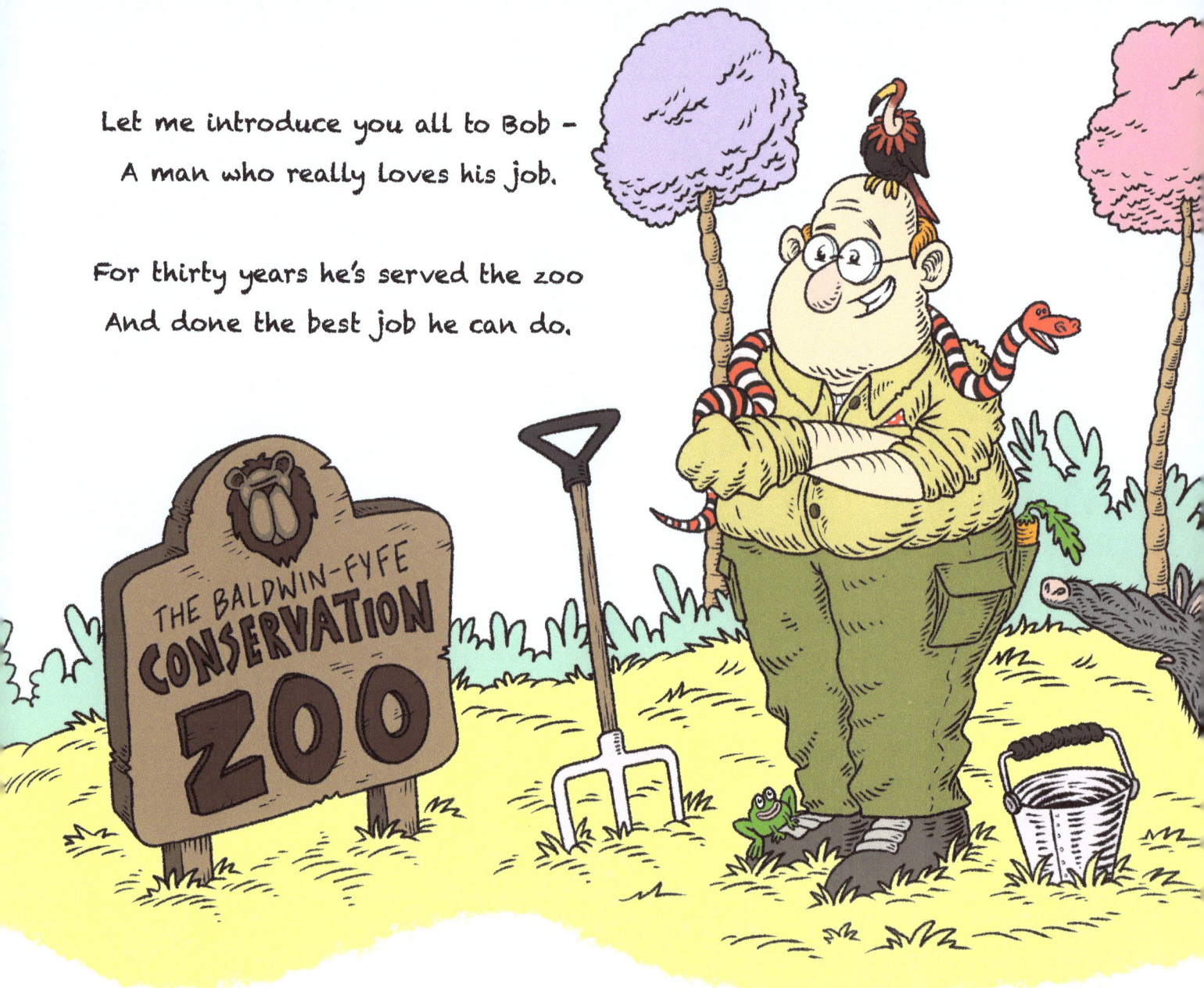

THE BALDWIN-FYFE
CONSERVATION
ZOO

Mucking out the elephants?
Bob does that with ease!

He even does the laundry
For all the chimpanzees.

Bob can calm the rhinos
And brush the lions teeth.
Once, he camped out in the gift shop
And caught the snow globe thief.

It's early on a Monday morning
Just like any other day.
Bob's tending to a poorly zebra
Feeding him some hay.

When, suddenly, Bob's walkie-talkie crackles into life
And he hears the voice of Zoo Director, Edgar Baldwin-Fyfe.

"Bob, come to my office
If you can please, right away!
For, we have a very special animal
That arrived here just today."

Quick as a flash
Bob makes his way there.
He walks into the office
And pulls up a chair.

"Thank you for coming."
Says the big, jolly man
In a patchy tweed suit
With a pencil in hand –

E. BALDWIN-FYFE

And hanging on to the pencil
Purple, blue and tiny -
Is the strangest little critter
Its eyes are round and shiny.
Its fur is spotty, its ears are floppy
It would make the cutest pet -

A floppy eared
Fluffy tailed
Pygmy marmoset!

Bob stares at the critter
Which stares right back at him.
"It seems as though she likes you!"
Says Bob's boss, with a grin.

"The zoo is home to animals
Of every shape and kind.
Some are fairly common
While some are hard to find.
Then there are the rare ones
And those, even rarer yet –
But this creature here before you
Is as rare as rare ones get."

"The floppy eared
Fluffy tailed
Pygmy marmoset!"

COMMON   RARE   AS RARE
AS THEY GET!

" She's from a distant island
Just east of the Bahamas
But she washed ashore, not far from here
In a crate of old bananas. "

" She used to have a family
But now she's all alone
So it's ever so important
That we make her feel at home.

She'll be living in the treehouse
Beside the pangolin.
I'd like for you to drive her there
And make sure she settles in.

But Bob, I should first warn you
This little critter's very bright -
And her favourite game is hide and seek
So don't let her out your sight.
If you look away for just one second
That could be too long
But I know that you can handle it -
I'm sure nothing will go wrong. "

With that, Bob's boss holds out his pencil
And leans forward, with great care.
Then the little critter hops across
And scampers up Bob's chair.
She clambers up his grubby sleeve
And then she comes to rest -
Clinging to his hanky
In the pocket on his chest.

"I won't let you down" Says Bob
"I'll guard her with my life."
Then he bids farewell, and waves goodbye
To Edgar Baldwin-Fyfe.

ZOO
DIRECTOR

Before he leaves, he peeks inside the pocket on his chest –

A fast asleep
Gently snoring
Pygmy marmoset!

Bob is on a mission
He's zooming through the zoo.
He whizzes past the lions
And past the cockatoo.

"Almost there" he thinks out loud
As he feels now is the time
To check his pocket passenger
And make sure she's doing fine.

But in the teeny tiny moment
He looks down from the trail –
A peacock steps in front of Bob
And opens up his tail!

LIONS LAIR

Suddenly Bob sees him
And overcome with fright
He grabs onto his steering wheel
And heaves it to the right.

His buggy hits a conker
And flips into the air –

And Bob comes tumbling out the side
Onto his derrière.

Dizzy and confused
Bob climbs up off the ground.
He checks inside his pocket
But there's nothing to be found!

He spots a flash of purple fluff
Out the corner of his eye.
Something scampers up a nearby tree
Into the canopy up high.

"There you are!" Bob cries out
As he makes off in pursuit
But the critter jumps out of the tree
Straight down a feeding chute.

Bob dives in right after her
Without a second thought.
There's nothing that he wouldn't do
To get this critter caught.

Elephants are everywhere
When Bob flies out the chute.
It's a good thing that he landed
On all that squishy fruit.

Standing up, Bob looks around
And gives his head a rub -
Then he spots the pygmy marmoset
Atop a spiralled shrub.

But Blue, the big bull elephant
Lets out a mighty sneeze
And the little critter's blasted off
Towards the chimpanzees.

Now Bob finds himself
Amongst the troop of chimpanzees
Doing what they always do –
Exactly what they please!

"What's that over there?" Says Bob

"Inside the tyre swing"

"The pygmy marmoset!" He shouts

"Don't move, I'm coming in!"

But before Bob has the time
To hurry over there
Koko drops down by the swing
And Koko doesn't share.

Koko gives the tyre swing
One almighty push
And the Pygmy Marmoset is launched
Beyond a great big bush.

After crawling through the shrubbery
And getting twigs stuck in his ears
Bob rises, to be greeted by
Two lofty, spotted rears.

Maggie is the tallest, off all the zoo's giraffes
And what's that on her head up there?
Bob cannot help but laugh.

Clinging to the bumpy bit, on top of Maggie's head –

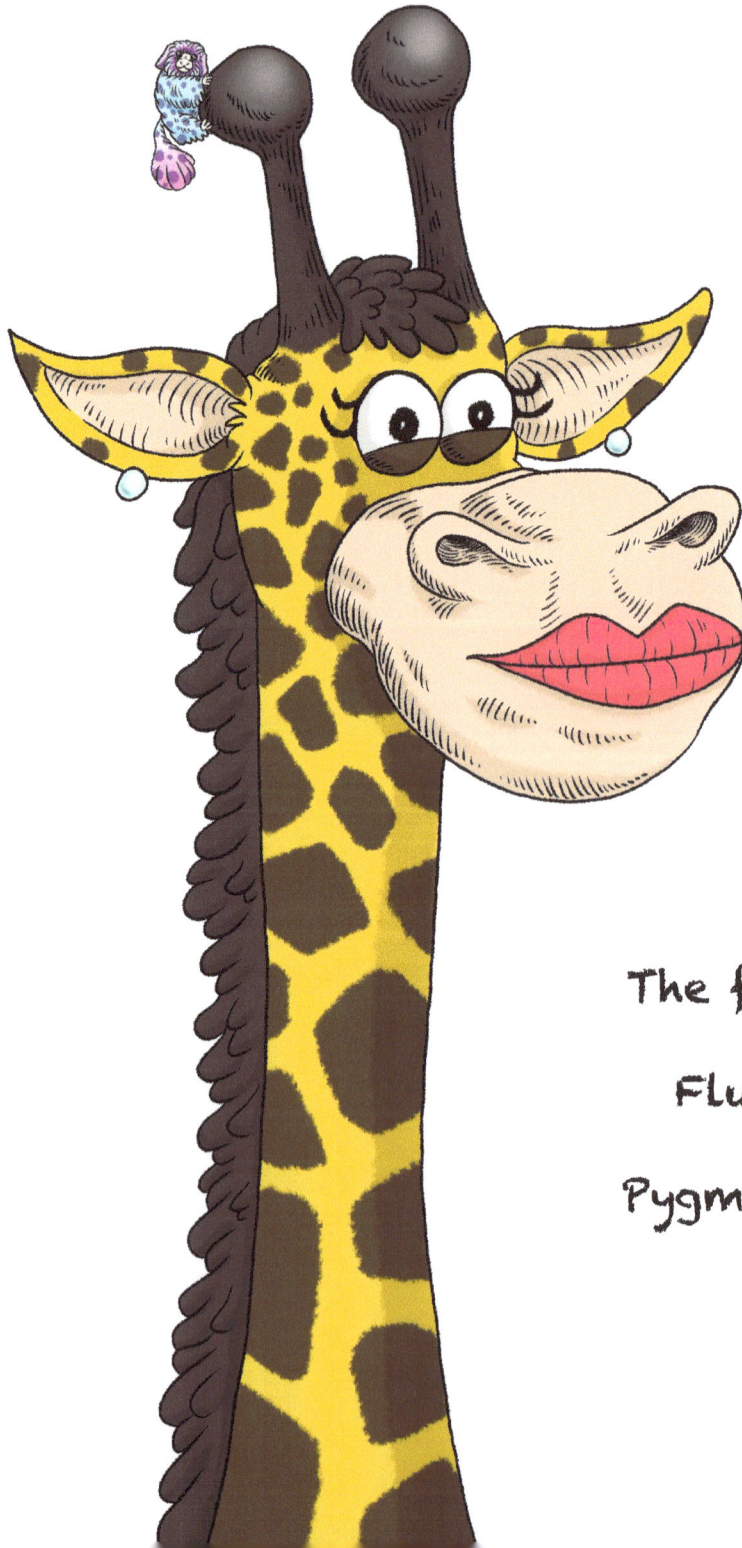

The floppy eared

Fluffy tailed

Pygmy marmoset!

Bob is far too little
To reach up there and grab her
Instead he has to call upon
His multi-purpose ladder.

But when he's only reached the height
Of Maggie's knobbly knees
Somewhere a balloon goes 'POP!'
And Maggie promptly flees.

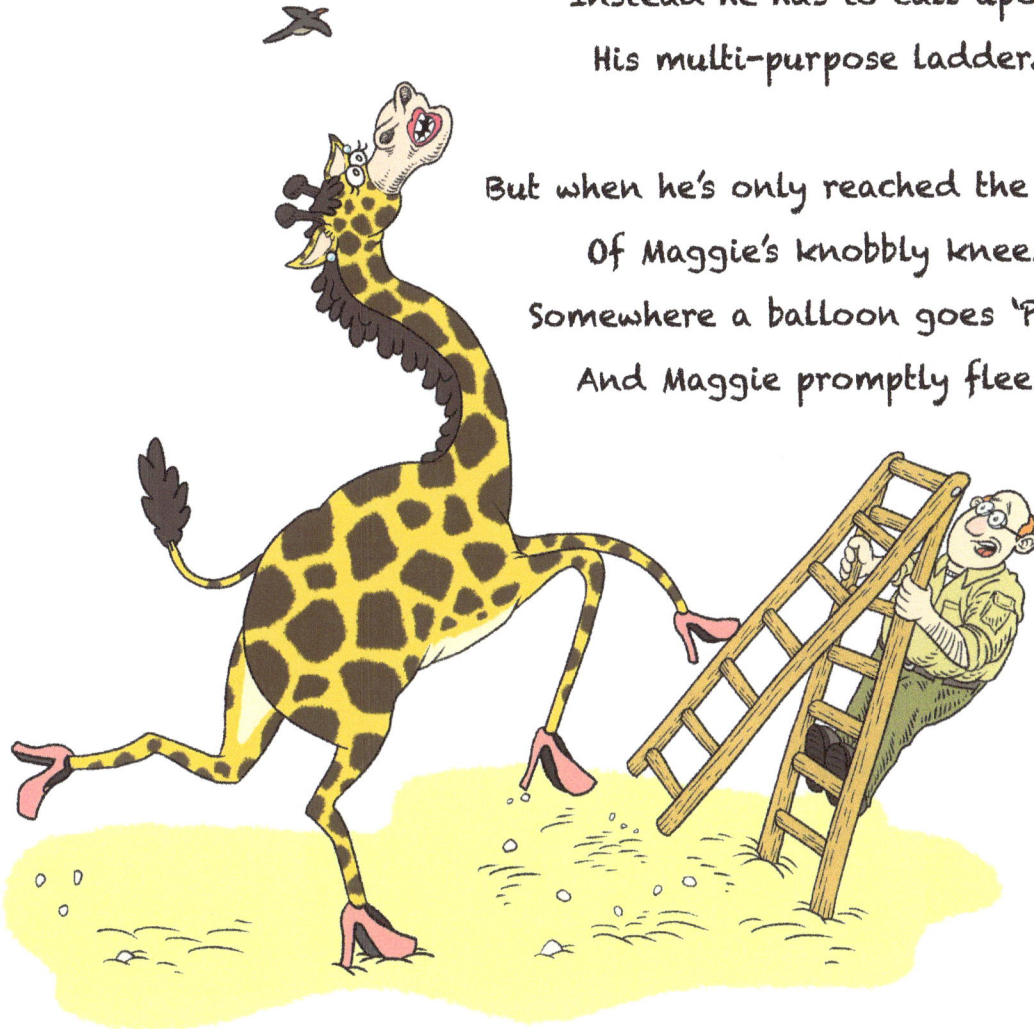

There goes the marmoset again
Up into the breeze.
Clinging to a helpful bird
That was eating Maggie's fleas.

Bob keeps the critter in his sight
'Till she decides to drop -
Landing in the penguin pool
With a tiny little 'plop!'

The penguins are relaxing
And having lot's of fun
Zooming down their water slide
And swimming in the sun.

" Where are you little Marmoset
I wish you wouldn't hide!
Is that you, all the way up there?
No! Don't go down the slide! "

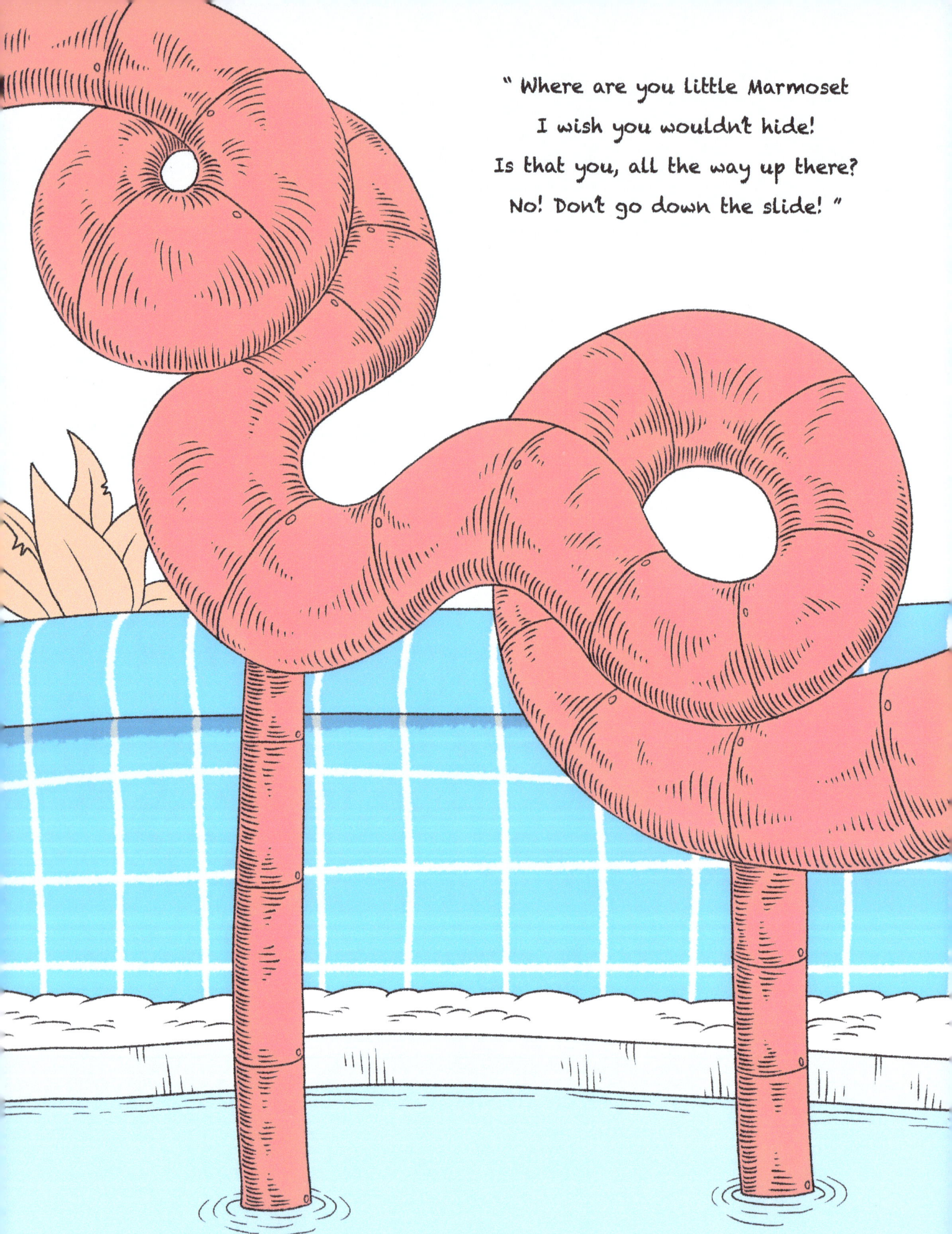

Bob watches as the Marmoset

Flies up into the air

And bounce straight off a penguins bum

Towards the lion's lair.

The lions are all sleeping
Which they do for most the day
Except for all the lion cubs
Who only want to play.

CAVE ♥SWEET♥ CAVE

HOME IS WHERE THE PRIDE IS

STRIPES MAGAZINE

"Please come back!" Bob cries out
But he gets no reply.
Overhead, dark storm clouds
Start to gather in the sky.

Seconds turn to minutes
And minutes turn to hours
All the lions have gone inside
To shelter from the showers.

But still, Bob cannot find her
This time she's truly lost.
"I've let everybody down" says Bob
"What will I tell my boss?"

Suddenly, Bob's eye is caught
By a soggy little rabbit.
Bob must of dropped his hanky
And the cheeky bunny's nabbed it!

The rabbit bounces here and there
It's floppy ears aflap
Then it disappears beyond the fence
Through a hidden gap.

Bob crawls through right after it
On his hands and knees.
His bottom nearly gets him stuck
He really has to squeeze.

When Bob pops out and looks around
On the other side –
He sees a secret beach ahead
And hears the lapping tide.

On the beach are gulls and crabs
Plus a couple on a date –

And washed up on the shoreline
A battered wooden crate.

Curious, Bob takes a look

At what's inside the crate.

He sees a pile of old bananas

In a soggy, rotten state.

But there's something else that Bob can see

Amongst the buzzing flies

A speck of blue and purple fluff

With four round, shiny eyes...

One of them is tiny
The other's even smaller yet -
Cuddling with her baby
It's the pygmy marmoset!

"I get it now!
It all makes sense!
That's why you ran away -
You were looking for your baby
You've been kept apart all day!"

Bob crouches down beside the crate
And offers out his hand.
"It's time to head back to the zoo
I hope you understand."

PANGOLIN

PROPERTY
TO LET

The trio reach the treehouse
Beneath a crimson sky.
Bob's happy to have made it here
Now it's time to say goodbye.

"Here we are then, little ones.
I'm sure you'll like it fine."
The Marmoset hops off his hand
And clambers up a vine.

She climbs up to a tiny door
But before she goes inside
She turns around and looks at Bob
And thanks him with her eyes.

I think they will be happy here
And get the best care they can get –
The floppy eared fluffy tailed
Pygmy marmosets.

The End.

Activity page

If I had a pygmy marmoset I would call it:

Checklist

Can you find everything from the list below?

An elephant shaped bush ☐   A carrot ☐
A baby turtle ☐   A brown mouse ☐
5 Snow globes ☐   A watermelon ☐
A cherry cup cake ☐   A bunch of balloons ☐
4 Sea shells ☐   A peg (to stop the smell!) ☐
A toy dinosaur ☐   The Queen of hearts ☐
An orangutan ☐   A green frog ☐
A rubber flamingo ☐   A deck chair ☐
A tennis ball ☐   2 Crabs ☐

Can you draw a
floppy eared
fluffy tailed
pygmy marmoset?

Try it here!

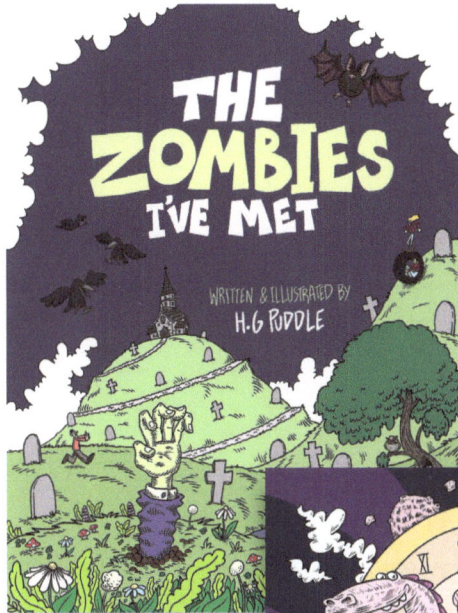

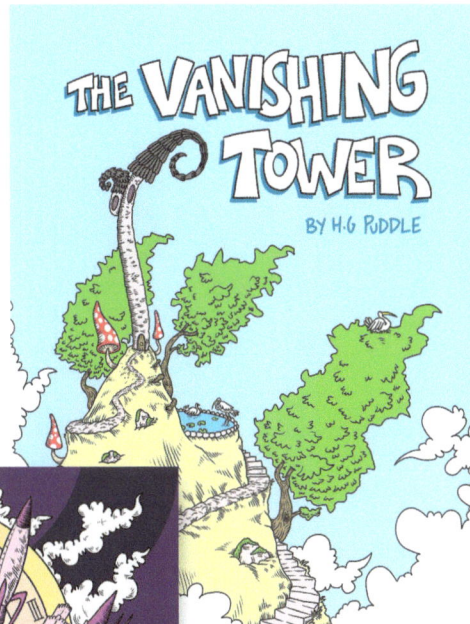

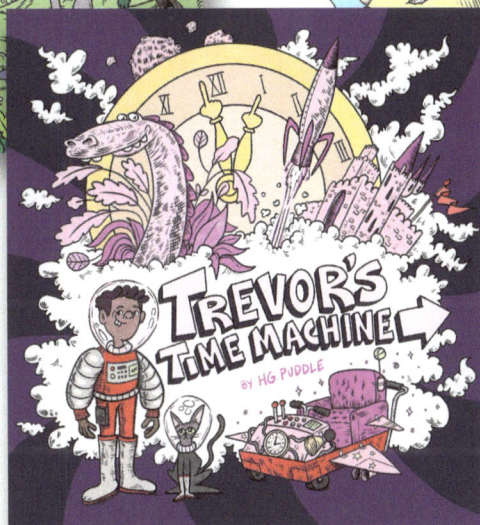

www.ingramcontent.com/pod-product-compliance
Lightning Source LLC
LaVergne TN
LVHW072125070426
835511LV00003B/87